C0-AWM-066

FORGERS *and* FORGERIES

BY *W. G. Constable*

CURATOR OF PAINTINGS

MUSEUM OF FINE ARTS, BOSTON

ART TREASURES OF THE WORLD

NEW YORK AND TORONTO

Copyright 1954 by Harry N. Abrams, Incorporated. Copyright in the United States and foreign countries under International Copyright Convention. All rights reserved under Pan-American Convention. No part of the contents of this book may be reproduced without the written permission of Harry N. Abrams, Incorporated. Printed in U.S.A.

701.18
A78
v.14

W. G. CONSTABLE

William George Constable was born in Derby, England, in 1887 and educated at Cambridge University and the Slade School of the University of London. He was formerly Assistant Director of the National Gallery, London; Director of the Courtauld Institute (University of London); and Slade Professor of Fine Art at Cambridge University. Since 1938, he has been Curator of Paintings at the Museum of Fine Arts, Boston.

The author of numerous books and magazine articles, Mr. Constable has devoted himself particularly to the study of English and Italian paintings and drawings. This is reflected in his more recent publications: *Venetian Painting* (1950); a monograph on the English artist Richard Wilson (1953); and *The Painter's Workshop* (1954).

THE USUAL IDEA OF A FORGERY IS of something deliberately fabricated to appear to be what it is not; something conceived in sin, and carrying the taint of illegitimacy throughout its existence. In fact, however, many things made for quite innocent and even laudable purposes have been used to deceive and to defraud, by means of misrepresentation or subsequent manipulation. So the essential element in forgery lies in the way an object is presented, rather than in the purpose that inspired its making.

Still, it is objects made to deceive which have always held the center of the stage. Without doubt, the main motive for their manufacture is to make money. But often there is an element of drama, even of romance, in the way they come into existence. A famous example is a *Sleeping Cupid* which the young Michelangelo is supposed have carved in imitation of the work of classical antiquity and which, after being buried in the ground, was bought by a dealer and sold as an antique, being rated as such until its true origin was revealed. Though the element of deceit was present from the beginning, the primary purpose of the work was a challenge to the past; and it is significant that Michelangelo's early biographers counted the success of the imposition to

48328

his credit, since it proved that he could successfully rival the sculptors of Greece and Rome.

Such challenges to the past have undoubtedly inspired men who were or ultimately became professional forgers. This seems to have been the case with Giovanni Bastianini (1830–1868), the Italian sculptor. His admiration for early Renaissance Italian sculpture bred in him a spirit of rivalry which issued in the production of remarkable imitations to be exploited as originals through collaboration with a dealer. Alceo Dossena (1878–1937) also seems to have wanted to prove himself the equal of earlier sculptors, though later he knowingly embarked on the making of forgeries of medieval and Renaissance Italian sculpture, skillful enough to be purchased as originals by various museums. The case for conscious rivalry with the past is clearer with Rouchomovski, the nineteenth-century goldsmith, whose abilities, though sufficient to give him a reputation in his own right, led him to make the famous tiara of Saitaphernes, which was purchased by the Louvre as Greco-Scythian work of the third century B.C.

With other forgers, however, desire to confound connoisseurs and the learned world has been uppermost, generally bred by neglect or adverse criticism. So it seems to have been with Thomas Chatterton and his eighteenth-century imitations of medieval poems; perhaps it operated in the case of T. J. Wise and his forgeries of nineteenth-century pamphlets; and apparently I. F. Ioni, the Sienese painter and restorer, well-known for his forgeries of Italian primitive paintings, derived at least as much satisfaction from trying to take in eminent authorities as from the money he made. Certainly such motives inspired H. A. Van Meegeren, the most famous forger of our time. Van Meegeren, a dexterous painter, skillful in imitating others, did not receive the recognition to which he felt his gifts entitled him, and turned his talents to forging the great Dutch masters of the seventeenth century. In 1937 he achieved spectacular success with his sale to the Rotterdam museum for $200,000 of his *Disciples at Emmaus,* as an early work by Jan Vermeer. A vivid light is thrown on his motives by a remark he made in 1947 after his arrest and trial: "The *Disciples* represented the master-stroke in my plan for vengeance." Later, the desire to fill his pockets seems to have become paramount. A similar case may be that of the Piltdown skull, once thought to be the earliest surviving relic of prehistoric man. Recent intensive examination has proved that though the

LEFT: A forgery by Giovanni Bastianini, part copy and part style imitation. RIGHT: A fragment of an original relief by Desiderio da Settignano on which the forgery was based.

cranium is of respectable antiquity, the lower jaw is that of a chimpanzee doctored to appear ancient; and there is some reason to think that it was made and planted near where the cranium was found, by a disgruntled museum technician who wished to prove that he could fool the learned world.

But whatever mixture of motives may go into making a forgery, the predominant one is almost always financial gain. It follows that what the forger makes is mainly determined by the market for his goods, which in turn depends on current activity among collectors and in the learned world. In the Middle Ages, fantastic curiosities and saintly relics were much in demand, and forgers saw to it that the supply was kept up. Later, the growth of scientific knowledge and religious skepticism spoiled this market; while recognition of the artist as an individual and the development of art collections stimulated production of forgeries imitating the work of particular artists or of particular epochs. These have since been the staple of the forger's trade, reflecting the tastes of the day. The eighteenth-century collectors' passion for classical antiquity helped to sustain in Rome a flourishing industry for the supply of classical statues and gems, with Thomas Jenkins, painter, art agent, and banker as one of its leading fig-

ABOVE: An example of a flourishing nineteenth-century industry: a forgery of a fourteenth-century Italian diptych, with (AT RIGHT) a genuine example for comparison. The crackle and facial types indicate the forgery.

ures; English Regency taste produced a fine crop of imitations of Sèvres and Meissen porcelain, made both in England and elsewhere; the Gothic revival, bringing in its train a new enthusiasm for Italian primitives, created hitherto neglected opportunities for the forger, who maintained an active sideline in keeping up the supply of Palissy ware and Italian majolica, until the taste of the

aesthetic period turned his attention to Delft ware; and in our own time we have seen the forger swing from fabricating Famille Rose and Famille Verte to meeting twentieth-century demands for the art of the T'ang, Sung, and earlier Chinese dynasties.

Just as he responds to changes in taste or in learned activity, so the forger follows in the footsteps of the tourist, for whom he has provided flint implements to be discovered in prehistoric sites; Greek and Roman coins, gems, and statuettes at appropriate places in Italy, Greece, and Asia Minor; scarabs and small sculpture in Egypt; and today, pottery and figurines in Central and South America.

Nor does the forger confine his attentions to the art of the past, but extends them to contemporary work. Constable and Corot were imitated while they were still living; forgeries of Renoir, Degas, Picasso, Matisse, and others are common today; while, among Americans, Winslow Homer and Ryder fabrications circulate freely. Artists are apt to be forgetful as to what they have produced, especially in the case of sketches, and have been known to deny authorship of perfectly genuine work; so that risks of confrontation are not too great. With a contemporary artist recently dead, his work not yet fully known or catalogued, a vogue for collecting him fanned by a skillful entrepreneur, prices not so high as to provoke critical examination, and with not too many genuine examples accessible for comparison, the forger is in velvet.

The two main methods of making forgeries, manufacture and misrepresentation, are in practice often combined; but it is convenient to discuss them separately. The simplest type of manufactured forgery is the straight copy, although this has considerable disadvantages. In addition to the necessity of choosing the right materials, imitating the right technique, and giving a proper appearance of age, the risks of confrontation with the original are great in these days of systematic combing of collections, aided by swift and easy travel, by photography and widespread publication. Sometimes, the forger attempts to meet this risk of confrontation by introducing variations into a design, so that the forgery may pass as a version of the original. But even so, comparison of the two is almost inevitable, with the almost equally inevitable exposure of any defects in the copy. It is this risk that makes forgers prefer to copy objects that are types rather than those stamped with the individuality of some particular master. The strictly controlled design and iconography of much Byzantine painting, and its

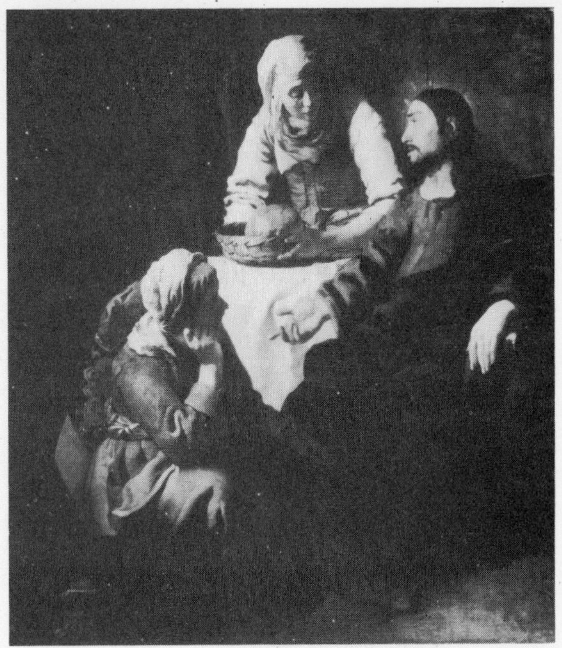

LEFT: A forgery of Vermeer by Van Meegeren, purporting to be an early work of the artist, purchased as an original, compared with (AT RIGHT) the earliest known painting signed by Vermeer.

standardized technique, encourages modern repetition; and the putting of one more copy on the market is not in itself likely to arouse suspicion. Similarly, the fact that eighteenth-century Chinese potters paid homage to those of earlier dynasties by making most admirable copies of their work, confuses the situation in favor of the forger. Another advantage (to the forger) of such objects is that many of them can be reproduced by casting. With some knowledge of the materials used for the originals and some skill in giving an appearance of age, such things as Chinese grave figures, Greek or Near Eastern bronzes, and coins can be produced in quantity. Sometimes, indeed, variation in the material of the cast is an aid to deception; as in the case of Renaissance bas-reliefs, when a cast in wax or stucco may, after some manipulation, be passed off as a sketch for a marble original.

More common than straight copies of particular objects, however, are imitations of the style of some period or master. This avoids the risk of comparison with a more or less identical original, and helps in passing off the forgery as an unknown example of the style it imitates. It was on this basis that Bastianini, Rouchomovski, and Dossena worked, as did the German painter Roerich in his

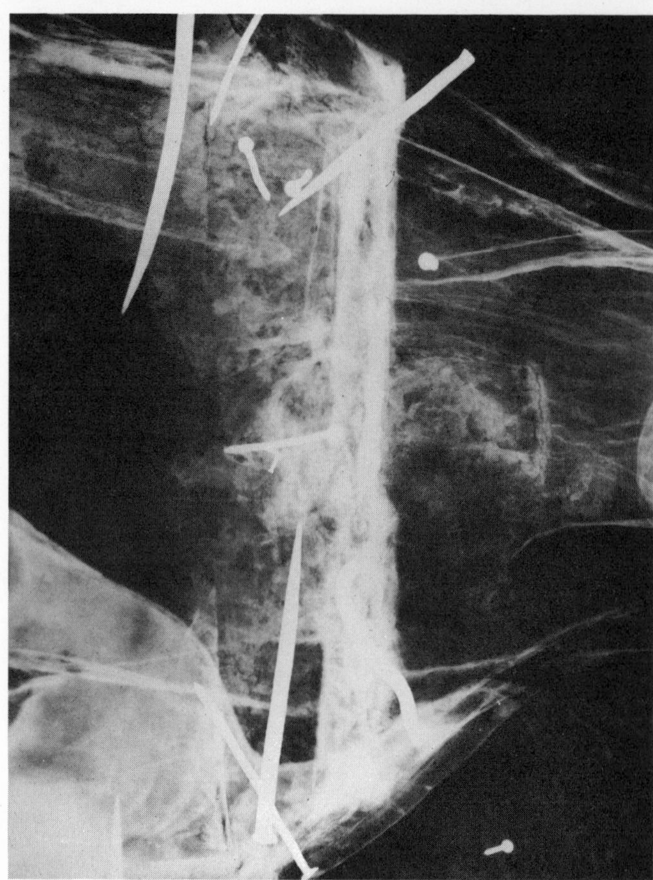

LEFT: A forgery of fourteenth-century Italian wood sculpture by Dossena. An X-ray (RIGHT) revealed modern nails in the interior.

imitations of Cranach and other early German masters. Usually such imitations of a style do not embody a new conception or an original idea; for the most part they consist of borrowings from original works, pieced together to make a more or less consistent whole. Often, these borrowings are secondhand, being taken from photographs, engravings, or reproductions in books. A specific case was the use of Weisser's *Bilderatlas zur Weltgeschichte* (1882) by Rouchomovski for the reliefs on the tiara of Saitapharnes. The use of such models is, however, the Achilles' heel of the forger. Once their source is tracked down, detection of the imposture is almost certain.

That, perhaps, is why forgers have on occasion virtually abandoned the use of models, either wholly or in part, and produced objects different from anything that is known, but which could fit into some particular historical or cultural background. Here, they are exploiting not only ignorant enthusiasm but the desire among the learned to extend knowledge of little-known epochs of human history, or to find material that will justify theories about them. Comparatively crude examples are the so-called Baphomets, stone figures said to have been worshipped by the Knights Templar; and the "medieval" pilgrim's badges made in nineteenth-century London by William Smith and Charles Eaton, now widely known as "Billies and Charlies." The appeal of the unknown was more skillfully utilized by Rouchomovski and Van Meegeren. In the tiara of Saitapharnes, existing models had been used, through reproductions, for the reliefs and inscriptions; but as a whole, the tiara was something of a kind unknown, yet eagerly sought for, and so was more readily accepted when it came into the market. Similarly, unknown early works of Vermeer had long been a matter of speculation among art historians, and in certain quarters a hypothetical character for them had been built up; so that when *The Disciples at Emmaus* appeared and more or less fitted the bill, it was all the more easy to believe in it.

A forgery of Egyptian limestone sculpture (RIGHT) compared with a genuine example of the type (LEFT). The forgery was proved so by analyzing the binding material of the color.

So far, the forgeries discussed have been substantially new constructions. This is to be expected when the motives of challenge to the past or self-vindication are at work; usually, however, the forger prefers to use a genuine piece, wholly or in part, as a starting point for his operations. This has none of the disadvantages of a copy; it avoids some of the difficulties of finding suitable materials; and it provides a pattern for such things as color, texture, and surface condition, in any changes or additions that the forger may make.

One possibility is to construct a forgery with the aid of genuine fragments, or on the basis of a damaged original. Joseph Nollekens, the eighteenth-century English sculptor, who worked with Thomas Jenkins in Rome, himself tells of making extensive additions to pieces of Roman sculpture found as the result of excavation, which in due course went into famous collections in England. Similarly, Dossena sometimes used fragments of genuine *quattrocento* work in his forgeries. This, too, was the method favored by Ioni for making his early Italian paintings. One great convenience of such procedures (for the forger) is that if suspicion is aroused and investigation made, it can always be alleged that the added work is merely honest restoration. Indeed, the line between restoration and forgery sometimes becomes blurred. Occasionally there appears in the art market a graft of a piece of one original onto another; its sellers would be consumed with indignation were it suggested that they had handled a forgery.

The exploitation of genuine work, however, often takes much simpler forms than that described above. The signature of a master may be added to a school piece, or to anything that bears some superficial resemblances to his work; sometimes, indeed, the addition is to a work by the master himself, to convince the doubting and to increase its sale value. Not infrequently, however, there is present an inconvenient signature of the real author, which has to be obliterated or manipulated into something more attractive. A special form of manipulation is to put on some anonymous portrait a name which more or less fits the dress and character of the sitter, and so increases its sale value. Shakespeare and Milton are often so honored; and many mediocre portraits picked up in England have been adorned with the names of Colonial worthies, and thus found a ready market in the United States.

All the examples of forgery so far mentioned are of the manufactured type, however little work may have been expended on them. In this they differ entirely from the forgeries which depend wholly on misrepresentation, a genuine

LEFT: A forgery (partly cleaned for examination) of a fifteenth-century Florentine portrait, compared with a genuine example (RIGHT). The forgery is on an old panel, but was finally proved false by the presence of titanium white, a twentieth-century pigment.

article of one kind being passed off as of another, without any physical change. It is not usual to brand such things as forgeries, and legally they are not so regarded; but morally, in that something is made to appear what it is not, they seem to be truly forgeries.

A simple and widespread means of falsifying in this way is a certificate of authorship and genuineness. Sometimes, the writers of these are of the highest competence and probity. These two qualities are not always combined, however; and the certificate then becomes either intentionally or innocently misleading. Unfortunately, most certificates are written for a fee, and there is always temptation for the writer to err on the side of pleasing his employer; while there is no question that sometimes certificates have been given deliberately to defraud. Moreover, forged certificates bearing reputable names are not unknown, a special variety being the stringing together of words from a genuine letter, with all qualifying or negative phrases omitted. There is, however, a more insidious method of giving a certificate, that of publication of an object in a reliable journal. Editors are generally careful enough; but they are defenseless in the face of a plausible case put forward by a name of some reputation, especially when the passage relating to the object is included in a more general context. This kind of certification is particularly difficult to cope with, since such articles will continue to be cited in later publications, perhaps mainly to controvert them but nevertheless renewing their availability for dishonest purposes.

Construction of false pedigrees is another means of misrepresentation, much used in the case of copies or versions. Sometimes, a pedigree is completely false, naming imaginary former owners whose existence cannot be proved but equally cannot be disproved. Sometimes, such history as the object may have is grafted onto that of another and accepted version, so that the two may become confused. A special case of this is the planting out of objects in houses whose owners are ready, for a consideration, to describe them as having descended in the family, or even as having been bought from the maker by an ancestor.

The skill, ingenuity, and knowledge of the forger and of those who exploit his work, are opposed to the skill, ingenuity, and knowledge of the collector and the learned world. The unaided human eye, if it has a trained and well-informed mind behind it, can go a long way in detecting forgeries. It is surprising how forgetful, careless, or ignorant a forger can be. He may employ materials whose inconsistency with the period to which his work claims to belong can be seen even by the unaided eye. More common is the introduction of such things as types and details of costume, or the use of coats of arms, that are later than the alleged date of the work. All such evidence, however, needs scrutiny, since it may simply be a case of later additions to a genuine object. More useful, therefore, may be tracking down the source of a forger's borrowings. If, for example, these at first sight seem to come from an original work, but follow much more closely the variations from that original in a later copy or engraving, the conclusion is obvious. Again, investigation of pedigrees, checking of literary references, searching through exhibition records, may all reveal suspicious or occasionally damning evidence of falsified history.

To tests based on observation and historical verification, we must add those mainly dependent on feeling. For the sensitive and trained observer, a number of indefinable characteristics will "add up" to a definite conviction of genuine

ABOVE: A forgery of a portrait by Cranach, and (BELOW) a genuine example. A style forgery, skillful, but coarser than an original.

or false. Qualities of surface and handling, subtleties in color and in the definition of form, the degree of unity in conception and treatment, and the emotional character of the work are among the things which influence such decisions. Thus, a copy, however exact, may reveal itself as lacking the coherence and the feeling which inspired the original; and the most skillful imitation of some older work may be recognized as a creation of its own time. Nobody can completely divorce himself from the prevailing thoughts, opinions, assumptions, feelings, and standards of his own period; and inevitably these will color whatever he produces, whether he be a forger or an original artist.

Scorn is often poured on judgments of the type described, and the expert who produces them in a court of law is the delight of the skillful cross-examiner. True, the only merit of snap opinions based on defective sensibility and inadequate experience is that they have a fifty-fifty chance of being right; but with sensibility backed by knowledge, an almost supra-rational instinct develops as to what is genuine or false. The so-called impression or hunch is, in such circumstances, more accurately described as a synthesis of many experiences. It is often forgotten that such almost instinctive judgments are not confined to art and archaeology. They play an important part in the sciences (where they are called hypotheses), in politics, in war, in business, and many other fields. Their value varies with the men who make them; but this does not lessen their potential value, and their occasional indispensability. In the detection of two particular types of forgery they are especially useful. Imitations of contemporary work can be very baffling, since the forger works with materials which were or might have been used in genuine work, does not have to give an appearance of age, and works against the same general background as does the artist he imitates. Similarly, a school piece which is misrepresented as the work of an old master, was produced in a similar physical and emotional environment. In such cases, a final verdict often has to be based on nothing but imponderable elements of style, realizable only through feeling based on knowledge.

The methods so far described of detecting forgeries may well be as old as the practice of forgery itself. Certainly, they form the basis of all investigations of which we have records, as well as of those made today. Their efficiency, however, has been immensely increased by the development of scientific methods of investigation. The first great step forward came with the use of photography, which permitted comparison of suspicious objects with genuine examples in a

ABOVE: An imitation of the work of John Constable, distinguished from an original (BELOW) by its coarse handling and mistakes in topography.

way hitherto impossible. Next came the application of various scientific techniques to the analysis of the physical constitution of an object. So spectacular have been the results in some cases as to create a blind faith in such methods of investigation, almost as though a piece of scientific apparatus were an oracle which when consulted would answer "Yes" or "No" to the question of whether an object is genuine. The limits of scientific investigation are, however, clearly marked. This method is solely concerned with the physical make-up of an object, and is completely indifferent as to who made it, when and where it was made, and why it was made. All that it does is to make possible the discovery of physical facts bearing upon these matters, which have to be observed and interpreted by human minds and used as the basis for human judgments.

The scientific procedures with which we are concerned here fall into two main groups. Of these, one includes various techniques for extending the range of human vision. The simplest is examination by microscope, which enables characteristics of a surface to be seen that would otherwise be invisible, so that,

OPPOSITE PAGE: A forgery of a painting by Utrillo adapted from a genuine example, compared with another genuine picture (ABOVE). Note the clumsy handling of paint and drawing in the forgery.

for example, painted cracks or cracks artificially induced can be distinguished from crackle due to age. With the microscope, too, evidence of removals and additions can be obtained, such as the manipulation of signatures and inscriptions, or the presence of repaint or artificial patina; while the structure of pigments, stone, etc., can be ascertained, as a step toward their identification. More elaborate is examination under various rays of the spectrum, to which the human eye is not sensitive but whose results can be recorded. The best known of these is X-ray, which penetrates certain substances but is held up in different degrees by others, especially metals, so that a photographic film behind an object will record a map of such substances in an object, thus revealing much that is below the surface. On the other hand, ultra-violet rays falling on a surface cause fluorescence, which varies according to substance and texture, so that additions to the surface may be revealed. Infra-red rays, in contrast, penetrate the surface, and are reflected back from the layers beneath, so that a photograph taken by infra-red light may reveal something concealed from the eye, which X-ray may not pick up.

The second group of investigatory methods includes various means of analyzing the materials present in an object. The most familiar is chemical analysis; but this is being supplemented and to some extent displaced by spectrographic analysis, with its recent extension in the use of X-ray diffraction. By these means, it is possible to detect even minute traces of substances whose presence or absence may be decisive in settling the date or provenance of a material. Some recent applications of quantitative analysis have proved helpful in ascertaining the date of objects. One of these techniques, determination of the extent of fluorination, was used to prove that the jawbone of the Piltdown skull was a modern forgery; while another, based on the amount of radio-active carbon present, which is known to decay at a certain rate, is still in course of development, but promises to be most useful.

Thus, a formidable group of weapons are available against the forger. To be effective, however, the significance of the facts they bring to light must be understood. Decisive proof that an object is not of the period or by the hand to which it is attributed comes only through the discovery of facts which are not only inconsistent with the attribution but cannot be explained except by assuming that the attribution is wrong. For instance, the body of a work may contain a substance unknown at its ostensible date. Modern nails inside a piece of wood sculpture said to be of the fourteenth century; cobalt, unknown as a pigment until the early nineteenth century, in a painting attributed to Velázquez; and titanium white, a twentieth-century invention, in a portrait labelled fifteenth-century Florentine—these are all good evidence that the object is not what it is held out to be.

Moreover, the facts discovered always have to be controlled by reference to established standards. Structure revealed by microscopic examination must be compared with that of known substances; chemical and spectrographic analysis has to be checked by reference to a codified series of earlier tests; crackle on a surface can only be labelled as false if the nature of genuine crackle is known;